What Could It Be?

Mike Graf
illustrated by Gary Phillips

Look closer, look closer
Over here, over there,
At things on the ground
And up high in the air.

A buzzing sound
From a bunch of stripes.
Don't get too close . . .

Or else it is "Yikes!"

bumblebee

Dropping down from a thread,
From the top of a tree.
It's black and crawling,

What could it be?

spider

6

Thousands of legs
Walking along.
It will be a while,

Before it is gone!

centipede

I hear a buzz
Beside my ear.
What is that bug?

Get out of here!

mosquito

Hopping along,
From here to there.
In the water,

And everywhere.

frog

Searching for food,
And crawling around.
Working together,

Underground.

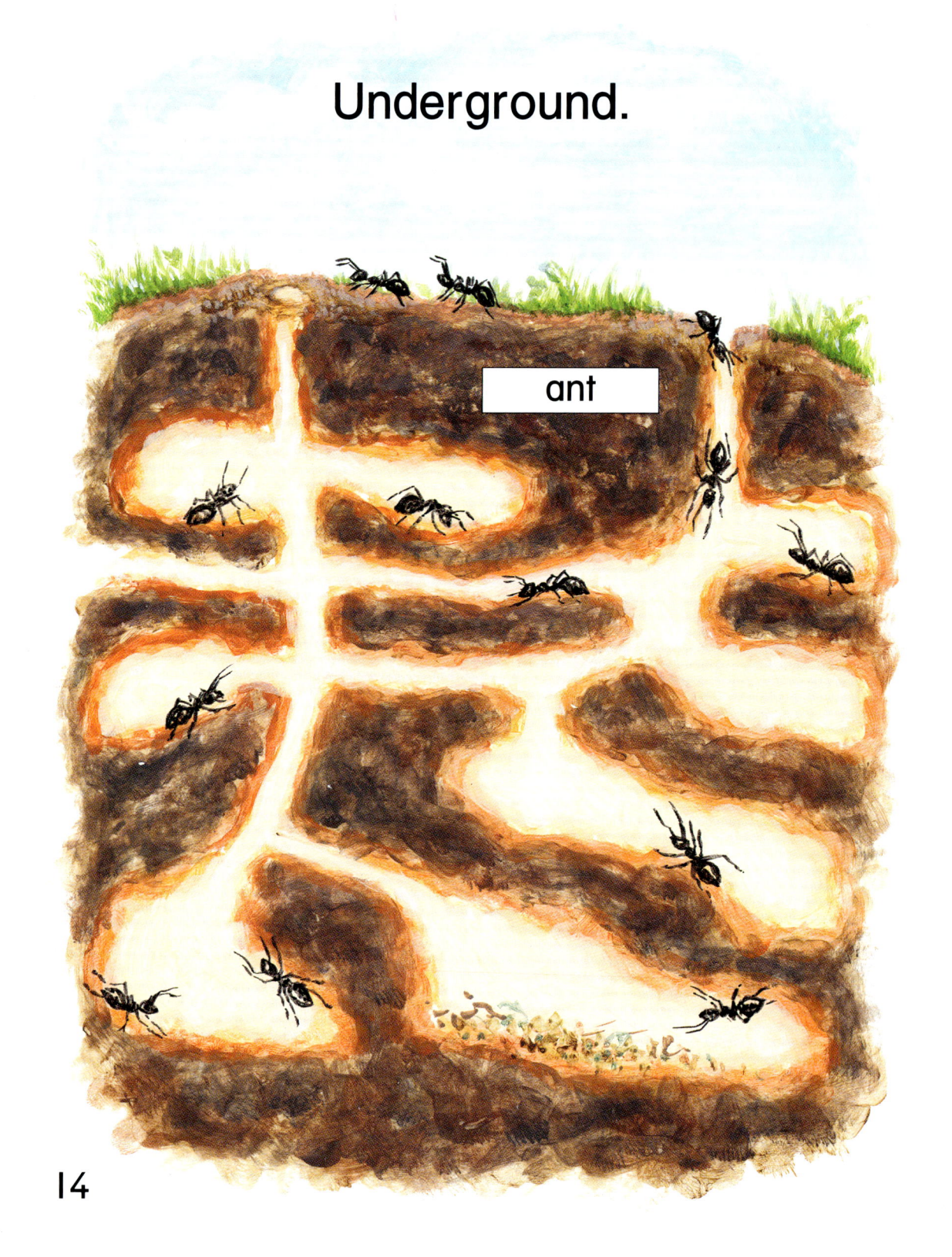

ant

Look closer, look closer
There's more to see still.
What will we find next
Over that hill?

16